P9-BZW-157

The Action of Subtraction

To my sister, Anne
—B.P.C.

The Action of Subtraction

by Brian P. Cleary
illustrated by Brian Gable

Millbrook Press / Minneapolis

Subtraction

is an action

that will make

your total less.

whether ice-cream scoops
or hula hoops
or inches from a dress.

Whatever
you are counting,
it will take away a part,

and leave you then
with not as much
as you had at the start.

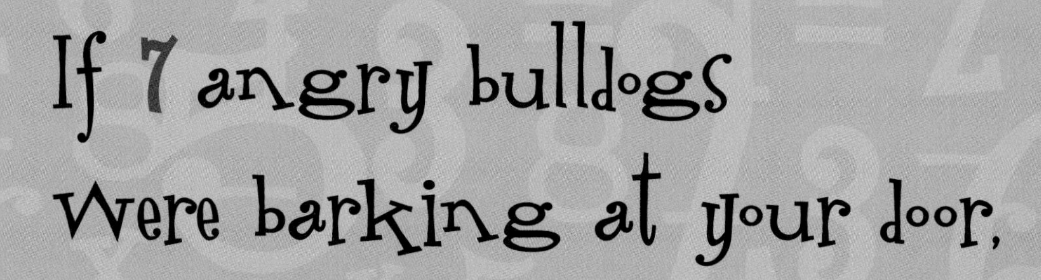
If 7 angry bulldogs
were barking at your door,

a kitten could scare 3 away.

Then you'd be left with 4.

And what if 13 hornets had nested in your tree?

If 10 of them would just buzz off,

you'd then have only 3.

Do you see what **subtraction** does?

It changes the amount,

So you'll wind up with fewer
when you do your final count.

"**Minus**" means to take away
some number from the whole.

Like if you had
10 bowling pins
and grabbed a ball to roll,

Let's say you knocked down 8 pins
with the first ball that you threw.

Then 2 would still be
standing 'cause

$$\begin{array}{r} 10 \\ \text{minus } 8 \\ \hline \text{is } 2. \end{array}$$

Your second ball knocks 2 more down.

You did it!

You're the hero!

Now all the pins are down because

2
minus 2
—
is 0.

In this case, "is" means "equals,"
or "totals just the same."

That sign means
matching value
in a problem or a game.

Like if you had 3 time-outs left
and somehow lost your shoe,

your coach would have to call 1,
and you'd be left with 2.

3 was what you started with.

Then you subtracted 1.

That would equal 2 more left before the game was done.

If Jenn had 12 stuffed animals, and she gave 2 to Sally,

then 5 more
went to Marykate,
here's how you'd do
the tally:

Start with 12. Take 2 away—

$$\begin{array}{r} 12 \\ \text{minus } 2 \\ \hline \text{is } 10. \end{array}$$

Subtract the 5 for Marykate.

Then that leaves 5 for Jenn.

Whenever we subtract things,
it can make us
sad or glad,

depending on
whatever there
is less of—good or bad.

Like fewer school days
due to snow
and less time with
the dentist,

not as much discomfort since
the doctor fixed your bent wrist.

A smaller plate of vegetables,
a shorter list of chores,
less time with your homework,

and not quite
as many
snores.

See!
The numbers move
toward 0
with a shrinking
kind of action.

And all of this is possible
because we have subtraction!

So, what is subtraction? Do you know?

5-3=2
HERO

Millbrook Press, Inc.
A division of Lerner Publishing Group
241 First Avenue North
Minneapolis, MN 55401 U.S.A.

Website address: www.lernerbooks.com

Library of Congress Cataloging-in-Publication Data

Cleary, Brian P., 1959–
The action of subtraction / by Brian P. Cleary ; illustrations by Brian Gable.
p. cm.
ISBN-13: 978–0–7613–9461–7 (lib. bdg. : alk. paper)
ISBN-10: 0–7613–9461–3 (lib. bdg. : alk. paper)
1. Subtraction—Juvenile literature. 2. Counting-out rhymes—Juvenile literature. I. Gable, Brian, 1949– ill. II. Title.
QA115.C54 2006
513.2'12—dc22 2005025881

Manufactured in the United States of America
1 2 3 4 5 6 — JR — 11 10 09 08 07 06